the Heart of Well-being

Seven
tools
for
surviving
and
thriving

A practical guide with audio CDs

*British Holistic Medical Association and
The Janki Foundation for Global Health Care*

The Heart of Well-being
Seven tools for surviving and thriving

The Janki Foundation for Global Health Care
449-451 High Road
London NW10 2JJ
United Kingdom
T +44 (0)20 8459 1400/9090
F +44 (0)20 8459 9091
E publications@jankifoundation.org
W www.jankifoundation.org

ISBN: 0 9548386 2 9

Cover and interior design: George Edwards
Illustrations: © George Edwards
Printed in Italy by Mediaprint

Author: Jan Alcoe

Jan Alcoe is a hypnotherapist, writer and trainer in holistic health and well-being. She was one of the core group that designed and wrote the training programme *Values in healthcare: a spiritual approach* (The Janki Foundation for Global Health Care, 2004). She is author of *Lifting Your Spirits: seven tools for coping with illness* (Janki Foundation for Global Health Care, 2008), which she developed following treatment for cancer. In this publication, Jan continues her journey towards discovering well-being.

Editor: Dr Craig Brown

Dr Craig Brown is a general practitioner and Chair of the British Holistic Medical Association. He is the author of *Optimum Healing* (Rider, 1998) and was one of the core group that designed and wrote the training programme *Values in healthcare: a spiritual approach* (The Janki Foundation for Global Health Care, 2004). He trains facilitators for that programme in the UK and other countries.

Acknowledgments

Su Mason for feedback on the draft book. Grace Fairley for copy editing and proofing, Bhavna Patani for production, administration and support.

To my family and special friends for their continuing guidance and inspiration.

Contents

This book is designed to be used with the accompanying CDs

Foreword

Dear Reader

Although most of us can visualise a state of well-being, it may seem more of an ideal than a reality. A pleasant 'spring-like' state of mind, harmonious relationships, good health and a life of abundance on all levels may be what we continuously strive to achieve, but the aim to live securely and comfortably has undoubtedly become a challenge in the present age.

Times have pushed everyone into chasing after a good life, a fulfilling career, and sustainable and committed relationships, but so often the outcome is stress, pain and ill health, rather than true joy and satisfaction.

Do we truly care for our 'selves' as much as we do our physical belongings, relationships and identity? Do we realise that we can definitely strengthen our own well-being irrespective of the situations we encounter in life?

Well-being can be a very soothing, gentle yet powerful state where the heart and mind are sustained by optimism, maturity, an open attitude towards the self and others, enthusiasm and much more. This is not an unrealistic aspiration and nor does it involve suppression of feelings or a controlled lifestyle. However, we do need to know how both the inner spirit and the body can be made to flourish.

With faith in goodness and determined thoughts, we can stabilise ourselves in a consciousness that is pure, unbound and loving. The vibrations that emerge can positively influence all that we do, promoting physical health and enhancing every relationship we encounter.

Commitment to change comes from realisation of the need to change. *The Heart of Well-Being* is a good companion for those on the path to complete wellness.

BK Janki
President
The Janki Foundation for Global Health Care

Well-being and health

It is common sense that how well we feel is going to affect how we approach life. Don't we all suspect, too, that we are more likely to get ill when negative influences outweigh our natural resilience? Once dismissed as old-fashioned, these ideas are beginning to be borne out by modern science. There is ever more research showing just how complete the mind to body connection is; that when one changes, so does the other. Happily, the balance swings two ways so it's not all bad news! Yes it's true that poor diet, lazy lifestyles and chronic worry will undermine our health but on the other hand, scientists are revealing the body-mind's built-in self-healing responses, and discovering ways of mobilising them. In future, we can expect doctors to be using the *well-being response* more and more for preventing illness and promoting better health and well-being; perhaps especially for people who have long-term health problems.

Jan's book leads us on a series of steps in this direction, and I believe that many people will find something of real and lasting value in her toolkit for well-being.

Dr David Peters
Professor of Integrated Health
University of Westminster

Introduction

Welcome to *The Heart of Well-being*. This book and accompanying audio CDs have been developed to help you learn about and improve your sense of well-being. They get to the heart of ways not only to survive but also to thrive, boosting your self-esteem, happiness and fulfilment.

This publication takes a unique approach to developing well-being. Not only does it explain why using certain tools will improve how you feel and how you approach life – physically, mentally, emotionally and spiritually – but it also provides opportunities to really *notice* how you feel and to *experience* these benefits in two ways: first, through simple activities and practices you can incorporate into everyday living; and, more unusually, through a collection of inspiring audio commentaries. The tracks enable you to relax, tune in and begin to experience the way that different aspects of well-being feel, as a basis for lasting personal change.

By using the book and accompanying audio tracks, you will be able to access personal resources that can sustain you through the usual daily routines, as well as through challenging times. The material has been designed with the following outcomes in mind:

- feeling energetic and well

- coping with stress, change and loss

- developing and sustaining healthy relationships

- improving self-confidence and self-care

- finding personal fulfilment and meaning in life.

As you dip into the guide and try out some of the ideas and approaches, you will find yourself taking an easier approach to life and enjoying the 'journey'.

Who this guide is for

This guide has been designed for everyone, because challenge and stress are ever-present in the fast-changing times in which we live. All of us find some days more trying than others, when we get out of bed on 'the wrong side', small hassles mount up and we lose our sense of perspective. Many of us suffer from work-related stress or have problems in health, relationships, family life or personal finances. Sometimes we may find ourselves coping with an unexpected change or trauma, for example, a redundancy, the end of a relationship, an accident or diagnosis of illness. Even positive experiences like holidays and new babies can have their stressful side. We may be aware of the toll that life events can take on us but be unsure of how to prevent the damaging effects this can have on our well-being.

As we respond to what is going on in the world around us our well-being can begin to become eroded without us even noticing. We forget what it is like to be fully well and we lose the sense of the potential we all have to achieve wholeness in our lives.

Whatever your personal circumstances, this guide will enable you to notice how you feel – physically, emotionally, mentally and spiritually. The information and practical exercises will then help you to protect and improve your well-being. Above all, the material presents a friendly challenge to:

- take a look at your current level of well-being
- try simple but effective ways of improving your well-being in all aspects of your life
- discover more about yourself and your inner resources.

What is well-being?

What words come into your mind when you think about well-being? Well-being or 'being well' is not the same as 'being healthy', that is, being without disease. In fact, here are some of the words people often associate with well-being:

vibrant, joyful, focused, creative, natural, free, connected, peaceful, optimistic, resilient, whole, grounded, centred, warm, happy, at ease, content, secure, balanced, decisive, clear, energetic, inspired, enthusiastic, relaxed, sociable.

As you can see, these words do not concern physical health, but rather a state that touches on many facets of our being. Even someone who is seriously or terminally ill can experience well-being. Whereas 'health' is about objective perceptions of our physical functioning, 'well-being' is more subjective – it is about 'how I *feel*'.

A sense of well-being springs from a number of different, overlapping dimensions in the way we experience ourselves and the world. It is fluid; our focus on each dimension can change from moment to moment and from day to day. However, by exploring these dimensions and how they interact, we can begin to arrive at what we feel is our own experience of *well-being*.

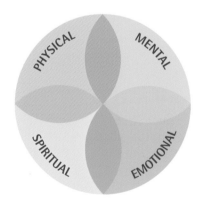

The **physical** dimension is the experience of our physical body, and incorporates physical energy, activity and functioning. It also includes how we use our physical senses of sight, hearing, taste, smell and touch to experience the world.

Factors to consider: physical health and functioning, fitness, vitality, strength, stamina, coordination, flexibility of movement, nutrition, sleep.

The **mental** dimension of well-being concerns the way in which we think and use our mind to make sense of what is happening around us, solve problems, develop strategies for action and learn from those decisions.

Factors to consider: concentration, memory, thinking patterns (positive/negative), mental/neurological health, capacity to solve problems, make decisions, set goals and plan.

The **emotional** dimension involves our very human capacity to feel – whether this is happiness, joy and contentment, or sadness, guilt and anger – and to understand and manage those emotions. Emotions arise in the most primitive part of our brain and are the precursors to thought and action.

Factors to consider: self-control, self-awareness, motivation, self-confidence, empathy (ability to read others' emotions), handling relationships.

Spiritual well-being is our ability to feel connected and, through this, to find meaning in our lives. We can feel connected with our inner selves by coming to understand the beliefs and values that guide us. However, spirituality is a journey of self-discovery that also leads outward. This may be expressed as a sense of connection with 'something' or 'some being' greater than the self: with family or community; with nature or with all living beings; with universal energy; or, through spiritual or religious practice, with God or the Divine.

Factors to consider: self-respect, self-expression, values and beliefs, contentment, sense of community and connection.

These four main dimensions of well-being overlap and interact, so that when we make a change in any one of them, this change will impact on the other three. A single negative event can spark off a whole series of negative events, as the examples below illustrate:

'When that driver cut in, I just got mad (emotional). I could feel my blood pressure rising (physical). I thought, "Right, I'll get him" (mental). I just couldn't recognise myself any more (spiritual).'

'When I eat junk food or drink too much alcohol (physical) I know it makes me drowsy and I can't think straight (mental). I then feel down (emotional) and can't see the point in anything (spiritual).'

'I worry about my workload and can't stop thinking about the things I have to do (mental). *My sleep suffers and I feel really tired in the day* (physical). *I get short-tempered with colleagues* (emotional) *and just don't feel part of the team any more* (spiritual).'

Alternatively, a positive change in one dimension of well-being can prompt a series of positive events in the others:

'When I started running again (physical), *I began to feel brighter and more motivated* (emotional), *so I was able to make a clear decision about the problems that were worrying me* (mental). *Now I feel I'm back in touch with myself and what is important to me* (spiritual).'

'I recently joined a choir and it's made me feel like I'm part of something again (spiritual). *The singing seems to have reduced the pain I experience from my arthritis* (physical) *and all the laughing we do has given me a lift* (emotional). *I'm even beginning to get my head around reading music* (mental)!'

'When I remember a happy time we had together (emotional), *I start thinking more positively about the relationship* (mental), *I feel closer to my partner and everything we have together* (spiritual) *and I really start to relax* (physical).'

In order to experience well-being, we can see that each of the four dimensions needs to be addressed so that we can create a balanced whole. If we are physically unwell, we can still redress the balance by enhancing our well-being on the emotional, mental and spiritual levels. Well-being is essentially about how we relate *inwards* to ourselves and come to understand ourselves through the four dimensions.

There is a further dimension of well-being, however, which is how we relate *outwards* – to others, our community and our environment.

When our well-being is compromised, we can withdraw, experience isolation and become more self-centred in our thoughts and actions. On the other hand, when we experience a sense of well-being, we feel more in touch with the needs and welfare of other individuals, our communities and our environment. We can then act in a way that expresses our higher values and, in doing so, feel fulfilment and meaning in what we do, as the following example illustrates:

'The main thing I do to sustain my well-being is exercise (physical), *particularly windsurfing. When I'm windsurfing I switch off from all the stress of studying* (mental) *and let go of upsets and frustrations* (emotional). *I like being in the water and sometimes feel a deep connection and oneness with nature* (spiritual). *I've met new friends through windsurfing* (community) *and we have formed a group to protest against pollution at sea* (environmental).'

There are many books about how to achieve optimum well-being; some talk about how the words 'health', 'holiness', 'healing' and 'wholeness' all come from the word 'holy'. This suggests that real health or well-being is a spiritual experience that arises out of self-knowing. Well-being springs from a sense of balance and wholeness whereby all the above dimensions come together and we begin to experience our more 'authentic' selves.

When we are conscious of this sense of wholeness, we lose our fear because we come to know who we really are. The tools and practices introduced in this guide are designed to reveal the centre of the well-being circle – the authentic 'I':

What challenges our well-being?

Life is full of ups and downs. The 'ups' can range from pleasant surprises to major changes we have sought out, like a promotion, moving house or having a baby. Even positive events like this disturb our equilibrium and can be challenging to cope with. The 'downs' can occur when we are just having a 'bad day' but may also involve unwanted change and loss, for example, the end of a relationship, a serious illness or the death of a loved one. We can find ourselves experiencing a rollercoaster of emotions that may, in turn, cause physical and mental difficulties and a sense of isolation and hopelessness.

When we look at all the changes going on in the world today, we see how these can impact at a personal level. Changes in society, politics, the economy, education, work, information technology, health issues, family structures and so on, all place demands on us to adapt and respond continually if we are to stay well and lead fulfilling lives.

In this increasingly complex and fast-changing environment, we can find it difficult to meet our basic human needs for attention, love, safety and control. We may try to meet our needs in inappropriate ways, and we see the results of this all around us in terms of sickness absence and burn-out at work, drug and alcohol addiction, obesity and eating disorders, depression, relationship breakdown, and anger and violence in the family and community.

Developments in media and communications mean that we are bombarded with negative news – news of war, violence, abuse, scandal, broken relationships, poverty, ill health and loss. We are also presented with an ever-increasing range of views, beliefs and values, which may further challenge or confuse us.

Many people say that the only certainty about life is that there will be uncertainty and change. When we cannot cope with change or feel that our well-being is beyond our control, we become more past- or future-focused as we remember what we used to have (the good old days) or focus on some vague and better future (it will all be alright when...). When we stop living in the moment, we lose the sense of meaning in our lives. We become less in touch with both ourselves and others.

As we continue through life, each challenge and change can become an additional 'knock', weakening our resilience on all levels of well-being. So how can we stay in tune with our inner selves and keep unnecessary suffering at bay? How can we boost our resilience and come to appreciate the journey life takes us on?

Change and opportunity

Many people who have experienced serious illness or major loss comment on how this has offered some unforeseen and positive benefits in their lives. When we are challenged by life, we can recognise the opportunities such changes bring with them. These commonly include opportunities to:

- reflect on our life situation and change our priorities in positive ways

- develop more meaningful relationships with partners, friends, family and colleagues

- learn new skills

- learn about ourselves

- deepen our spiritual awareness and practice.

Surprisingly, challenging situations can present us with unexpected moments of fun, happiness, peace and fulfilment, which arise from a growing ability to live in the moment. Freed up from the responses that are triggered by anger and fear, we can behave more flexibly and begin to see things in perspective. We discover personal strengths and qualities we didn't know we had. These can help us to cope with the change and challenges we face in constructive ways, and to find a new sense of balance and well-being. As we learn more about ourselves at a deep level, we begin to connect more meaningfully with others, our communities and our environment.

What supports our well-being?

The purpose of this guide is to help you to discover a way not just to survive the knocks in life, but to positively thrive and enhance your well-being on every level. The guide introduces some tools for well-being that you can begin to experience in your day-to-day life. In particular, these tools will help you to find and draw upon a quiet place of strength and sustenance inside yourself. While you may be dealing with uncertainty, anxiety or the distress of others, tapping into this inner sense of resilience will give you a more balanced perspective on what is happening. You can then think and act in ways that are most beneficial for your well-being – physically, mentally, emotionally and spiritually.

The seven tools are:

1. **Relax and tune in**
2. **Use your imagination**
3. **Think positively**
4. **Be creative**
5. **Lighten up**
6. **Value yourself**
7. **Discover peace**

They are all simple practices that you can incorporate into your daily life (both at home and at work), often for as little as a minute or two. The particular benefits of regular practice may include:

Physical:

- enhanced physical health and immunity
- improved vitality and sleep

Emotional:

- reduced anxiety and distress
- ability to stand back from difficult situations and react in a more resourceful way

Mental:

- clear, positive thinking and decision-making
- creative problem-solving to overcome barriers and difficulties

Spiritual:

- learning more about who you are and recognising your inner values and resources
- increased contentment and a sense of connection with something 'greater' than yourself.

One of the most exciting outcomes of using these tools is that they help us to discover who we really are – without the layers we wear when we play our many and varied roles in life, and without the teeming and often trivial thoughts that occupy our minds. We discover a more authentic 'being' within ourselves, which can begin to have a voice in what we feel, think and do. In fact, we start to feel whole again. It is this sense of wholeness that helps us to stay resilient in the face of everything that life brings and discover lasting happiness.

How to use this guide

The guide consists of a book and two audio CDs.

The book begins with an easy way of establishing your baseline of well-being – how you feel now. It is helpful to take a few minutes to complete this, so that you can measure your progress as you work through the rest of the material.

Each main section explores one of the seven tools, and contains:

- a short introduction to the tool and the benefits of using it

- reflections from people who have practised using the tool in everyday life or during challenging times

- some activities to help you to notice how you feel and practise using the tool during your day, including ideas that will only take a few moments of your time

- reference to a track on the audio CDs that you can use to experience the essence of the tool in action and to deepen your practice.

At the end of the book is an opportunity to reflect on any changes you have made and to develop your plan for lasting personal well-being.

The CDs contain simple, guided visualisations that you can use to relax yourself and deepen your experience of the power of each tool. You can play these at any time (except when you need to concentrate, such as while driving) and in any position (seated or lying). Use pillows or cushions to support your body in a restful position. Make sure you are completely comfortable and able to relax deeply for some time without interruption. (The approximate length of each track is given next to its title.)

Most of the tracks are designed to be deeply relaxing, and regular listening will help you to benefit in many ways. Don't worry if you drift off to sleep while listening to a track. You probably needed the extra rest. In time, you may find that you can focus on the content all the way through.

Practising

We suggest that you begin with the first tool, *Relax and tune in* (page 21), as the ability to relax and stay in tune with yourself underpins everything else you go on to do in order to enhance your well-being.

You can then feel free to choose another tool that feels right for you at the time. You can practise the tools in any order and can decide to use one or two you find particularly helpful, or all seven of them. Read the information in the relevant section of the book and then listen to the CD track that is signposted.

Try out some of the additional ideas for practice from the book over the coming days. Each section contains several practice activities, most of which will take less than an hour to try out. However, in each section you will also find a number of suggestions under the heading 'Moments of well-being', which will only take a few moments and which you can incorporate into your day with ease. If you do not have the energy or motivation for practice, don't judge yourself critically. Just do what you can and feel the benefits. Even if you relax to a CD track only occasionally, it will help to bring about positive change.

You might like to make a note of what you do and any changes you notice in your overall sense of well-being or in specific thoughts, feelings and behaviours. Above all, show appreciation to yourself for taking some positive steps towards enhancing your well-being.

How 'well' do you feel?

Before you embark on this journey towards well-being, it will be useful for you to know where your starting point is. How do you feel right now, in terms of physical, emotional, mental and spiritual well-being?

Below is a simple tool to complete in order to map out your current state of well-being. The resulting picture will enable you to spot areas you may wish to improve on or priorities for your well-being right now. It will also provide a record against which you can plot improvements as you begin to tap into the resources in this guide.

Remember that 'well-being' is a subjective state and so your own sense of well-being is what is important. How you rate your well-being will depend on factors and feelings that are important to *you*, so approach the exercise with intuition rather than the analytical mind!

Well-being audit

1. Overall rating

Begin by quickly and intuitively rating your overall sense of well-being from 0 (low) to 10 (high) and write down your score in the box at the top of page 18.

2. Rating each dimension

For a slightly more detailed rating of your sense of well-being, look at each of the four dimensions of well-being on the wheel on page 18 – physical, emotional, mental and spiritual. You can remind yourself of what each dimension covers by referring to pages 6-7 and the reflections under the heading 'What is well-being?' on pages 7-9. Notice that each dimension has ten levels (numbered 0-10), working out from the centre. Begin by quickly rating yourself from 0 (low) to 10 (high) on each dimension. Don't spend time analysing or thinking too much, just allow your intuition to find the right level.

Shade the resulting area in a different colour for each dimension. Now you have a picture of how 'well' you feel right now.

You might then like to consider some of following questions and make some notes to come back to:

⊛ Which is currently my strongest dimension of well-being? How can I maintain this level of well-being? How can I use it to influence and enhance my well-being in the other dimensions?

⊛ Which areas need most improvement? What difference will it make when I increase each of my ratings by 1? What impact will it have on the way I look, feel, think and act? What impact will it have on others close to me?

3. Vision of well-being

Finally, consider what it will be like when you achieve optimum well-being (a rating of 10 on every dimension):

⊛ What will I look like? What will I feel like? How will I think? How will I behave? What difference will it make to my personal life, my work, my relationships and any other important aspects of my life?

Develop this vision in your mind and write it down in the box on page 19. Let it be like a guiding star as you work your way through this book and CDs.

My current rating of overall well-being: ☐

My wheel of well-being

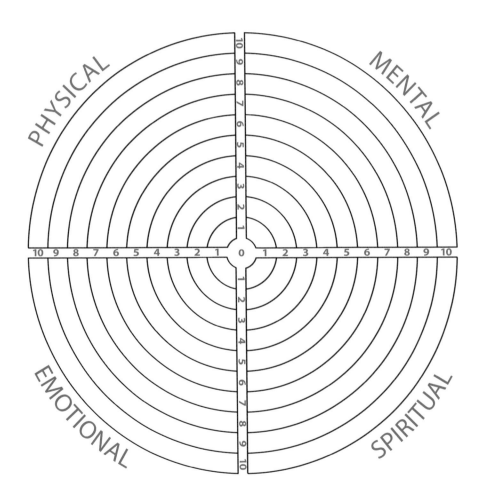

My vision of well-being

Tool 1

Relax and tune in

When I relax, I can take a step back and see the wood for the trees

It is a great feeling to be relaxed, calm and at ease. We can be more 'ourselves' and life seems more fun. Being relaxed enables us to be more positive, creative, flexible and tolerant. We can avoid getting too emotional about issues and problems that arise. We can think things through, make decisions we feel good about and put things in perspective. Learning to relax is the first step to improving our well-being on all fronts.

All humans have an in-built stress response. Like a burglar alarm, this is designed to keep us safe by 'sounding off' when we perceive a threat or danger to our safety. It mobilises our whole body to 'fight or flee' before we have time to think. It is a valuable thing to have for our survival, provided it turns on when we need it and off when we don't. Just like a faulty alarm, however, it can turn on indiscriminately, not because we are in physical danger but because, for example, we have worries about money or health, work deadlines or family upsets.

We might also imagine difficult situations that haven't even occurred, and fear that the worst will happen. Such thoughts will trigger the stress response, too, together with the physical effects it sets in motion: release of the stress hormone adrenalin, faster breathing, increase in heart rate and blood pressure, sweating and muscle tension. At the same time, our non-essential functions, like digestion, immune function and even logical thought, begin to 'shut down' in order to divert energy to where it is needed.

In today's fast moving world, the adrenalin rush that stimulates us into action can give us a useful edge when we are under pressure or need to pull out all the stops. Some people begin to depend on this regular adrenalin 'fix' to keep going, however, and so they keep the pressure on themselves and those around them, by setting themselves unrealistic goals, being perfectionists or trying to be the best at everything they do.

In the long-term, without regular rest and recuperation, the wear and tear begins to take its toll and the adaptive response that was designed for our short-term survival becomes counterproductive. A constant, low level stress response will eventually lead to physical problems like pain, exhaustion, a lowered immunity, and skin, digestive and blood pressure disorders. It will also impact on our emotional and mental well-being, causing sleep disturbance, poor concentration, worry, panic attacks and even depression. Trapped in the stress-related emotions of aggression, anger, impatience and fear, we find ourselves unable to meet our basic human needs and our

1

relationships suffer. As we begin to feel disconnected from life and those around us, our spiritual well-being is also impaired.

The good news is that the body and mind can cope with and recover from the effects of stress if we take action before serious damage is done. We can 're-set' our survival alarm and counter the tendency to 'live on our nerves' by learning to relax and tune in to our inner world. As we relax and turn away from the busy-ness of our surroundings, the relaxation response (the counter-mechanism to the stress response) is triggered; our muscles relax, our heart and breathing slow down, our internal organs work more efficiently and our body can find the deep rest it needs in order to repair. Biochemical changes in the brain are also triggered, which improve our mood, and our mind can become clearer. As we calm down, the high emotion that is attached to the stress response begins to calm down too. We then find that we are able to take a step back from situations that are causing us stress and see the bigger picture. We can observe ourselves and notice how we are responding.

Regular, deep relaxation can help us to change the way in which we think and act. We then discover that things we thought were important no longer loom so large and we can re-prioritise. We might decide that the emotion we were investing in a relationship or a pursuit is not necessary and we can take a more objective approach. As we bring relaxation and the quality of 'the observer' into our external world, we begin to deal with worries – both real and unfounded – more rationally. We avoid getting 'hooked in' to the emotions and dramas of other people and we stop creating our own! Most importantly, we can begin to meet our well-being needs in healthy and resourceful ways.

How to relax

Energy check

We all experience natural highs and lows of energy during the day, as the body needs to rest, dissipate any build-up of stress and recharge. Checking in at regular intervals helps us to notice when we feel tired or stressed, and taking a short, deep relax gives the body and mind that much-needed break. We then feel re-energised, physically and mentally, for the rest of the day.

1

Relaxation techniques

There are many simple techniques for relaxing quickly and effectively. For example, we can focus on our breathing or we can learn to contract and relax groups of muscles, working from our feet up to our face. Some relaxation activities are included at the end of this section and on the CDs. In addition, all the tools in this workbook will deepen relaxation practice.

Be 'easy'

Being relaxed is also about creating an attitude of 'easiness' with ourselves – developing an approach to life that is playful, forgiving and light towards problems (see *Lighten up* on page 59). When we start to get stressed, it is helpful to relax because this enables us to slow down and avoid acting too quickly. Changing our approach to life can seem difficult but if we treat it in a light-hearted manner, almost as a game, we will start to see results. If it works, we can do more of the same. If not, we can relax and try again.

Tune in

We can easily become distracted and mentally 'elsewhere', rather than truly present – aware of our inner selves and of how we are relating to our outer world. Learning to tune in and stay 'in tune' with ourselves, despite the demands going on in our surroundings, is a vital ingredient of well-being. Whenever we are confronted with choices and decisions, we can ask ourselves some key questions about what we do and how we respond: 'Does this feel good for me right now?' 'Does this enhance my well-being?'. We can be mindful of our bodies when we decide whether and what to eat or drink, when to rest and sleep, whether to walk that extra mile or stay up late studying. We can be mindful of our emotions, for example, when we decide whether to get upset about our friend forgetting to call or angry at someone's outburst. Being mindful of our own needs can then extend to the way in which we respond to others, as we bring an observing quality to our actions. We become more focused on the person or people we are with and can give them our full attention. We can be fully open and receptive, while staying relaxed and connected to our own inner world of well-being.

Live in the present

As we practise relaxation, we begin to live more in the present. We might notice that we become increasingly flexible and adaptive to changing situations. These qualities are important characteristics of people who are relatively stress-proof, and such people enjoy better physical and mental health than those who are more rigid, black and white thinkers. We do not have to feel that we are stuck with traits that make us prone to worry and stress. Attitudes, beliefs and behaviour can be changed, to the point that stress no longer seems so uncontrollable. All the tools in this guide will help you move towards this end. You will find some practices to get you started at the end of this section.

Benefits of relaxing and tuning in

Physical:

- encourages healthy choices about eating, exercise, sleep etc
- provides health-giving, deep rest for the body

Emotional:

- maintains a sense of calm in responding to life's demands
- enables us to observe ourselves and react to situations more resourcefully

Mental:

- fosters mental clarity and more robust decision-making
- helps us to develop a wider perspective on problems and challenges

Spiritual:

- allows us to develop a deeper understanding of the relationship between our inner and outer worlds
- improves our capacity to stay in tune with ourselves and others

1

Reflections

> I was feeling overwhelmed, as if my life was out of control. I started to over-eat because it was comforting and made me feel safer. It was only when I began to go to relaxation classes that my anxiety calmed down. I began to see that there were things in my life that I could take control of, and that I could meet my needs in healthier ways.

> I've developed the habit of stopping for five minutes at least three times a day. I go through each part of my body, from head to toe, checking for tension and imagining it softening and relaxing. I then take myself to a beautiful place in my mind, somewhere in nature where I can appreciate the shapes and colours, the sounds and the sensations. I can now do this really quickly, and afterwards I feel energised and ready for anything.

> I've noticed that there is a time of day when I just feel sluggish and tired. Because I work at home, I can take myself off for 20 minutes and have a deep relax, using a relaxation track or just focusing on relaxing my body. Having this deep relax, rather than just nodding off to sleep, is really restoring. It helps me get through the rest of the day feeling resourceful and calm, rather than tired and irritable.

How to practise relaxing and tuning in

 CD track

Take a deep daily relax using the following track:

CD 1 Track 1: Relaxing stream (14 mins)

You can also play any of the other tracks on the CDs to relax to.

1

Meet your needs

Stress often arises when we do not meet our innate physical and emotional human needs in appropriate and healthy ways. We can all benefit by reviewing from time to time whether and how well we are meeting these needs.

Below is a table that lists nine basic human needs.

1 To what extent are you meetingeach of these needs in your life right now? Give each need a score on a scale of 0 (low) to 10 (high).

Basic need	0	1	2	3	4	5	6	7	8	9	10
1. Having a sense of security and safety											
2. Giving and receiving attention											
3. Looking after the body (eg. through good diet, regular exercise, rest and relaxation)											
4. Having purpose, challenge and meaning in life											
5. Having a sense of competence and achievement in life											
6. Being part of a wider community and making a connection to something bigger than yourself (eg. through religion, community work, a club)											
7. Feeling understood and being able to share with someone (friendship and intimacy)											
8. Having a sense of control and autonomy											
9. Having a sense of self-esteem, status and recognition											

'Based on *Human Givens* (Ch.5) by J Griffin and I Tyrrell (2006, HG Publishing).'

2   Select one need that you consider is not being satisfactorily met at the moment in your life (eg. that you gave a score of less than 5).

3   What could you do differently that would increase your score by **one** point?

In reflecting on this question, consider tackling any underlying 'stressors' and deciding which of them can be changed, reduced or eliminated. These might include:

- internal stressors that arise within you, like poor diet, too little creative fulfilment, unresolved conflicts, painful memories, lack of consistency or rhythm in work or personal life, inability to notice signs of tension, tiredness or exhaustion

- external stresses that arise around you, like noise, people you find difficult, adverse work conditions, major life changes.

Now, how can you introduce more of the things that meet the need and make you feel good?

When you are ready, you can consider another need in the same way.

Activity audit

Here are some simple questions that are useful to reflect on from time to time:

- What activities make you feel more alive? **(Energy)**
- When do you seem most relaxed, as if you are really 'being yourself'? **(Authenticity)**
- What activities come most easily to you? **(Ease)**
- What activities do you simply love to do? **(Motivation)**

Then start to do more of what comes naturally to you.

Deep relax

Aim to set aside 15-20 minutes each day to give your body and mind a deep rest, following the guide below. Alternatively, use the CD track *Relaxing stream.* You will find that you feel energised and more focused for the rest of the day.

15-20 minute relax

If you are sitting, uncross your legs and place your feet on the floor. If you are lying, make sure your head and body are supported. If you have tension, aches or any pain, you will discover that the effects of relaxation will soon diminish or distract from these.

Put your hands on your abdomen and take three deep breaths in and out from this place. As you breathe in, your abdomen should rise, as if it were a balloon filling with air. As you breathe out, it should sink back. Do not force this, just allow the breath to come and go in an easy way.

Now focus gently on each part of the body, starting with your scalp and working through your face, neck, chest, arms, hands and fingers, upper back, stomach, lower back, pelvis and hips, thighs, calves, ankles, feet and toes. As you focus on each part, silently invite it to relax and to let go of any tension or discomfort. Alternatively, you can tighten each part and then let it go completely, noticing the difference between tension and relaxation.
Repeat this once more before moving on to the next area.

When you have worked down to your toes, rest quietly, keeping a soft focus on your breath rising and falling in your abdomen.

Tune in to an activity

Many people find that spending time doing something that requires them to focus their mind in a particular way is relaxing, for example, reading, doing a crossword puzzle, cooking or sewing. Others find relaxation in becoming absorbed in a physical activity such as fishing, swimming, running or playing sports.

Tune into your surroundings

Take a walk alone and notice everything around you. Notice the colours, the shapes, the textures and the quality of light. Notice any sounds, movement

1

or scents, and any sensations as you 'interact' with your environment – for example, the feel of your feet crunching on gravel or your body leaning into the wind.

If you are indoors, take time to tune in to what is around you in the same way. Again, notice the colours, the light, the texture and feel of the furnishings, the qualities of the objects in the room, the sounds and sensations – for example, the warmth on your skin from a fire, the scent of bath oil and the feel of the water as you sink into a bath.

Tune in to others

The next time you are with a friend, family member or colleague who wants to tell you something, quickly relax by letting go of tension in the body and breathing a little more deeply from the abdomen. As you calm down, allow your attention to be fully focused on the person you are listening to, really tuning into what they are saying, rather than allowing your thoughts to drift off. Notice how this deeper quality of listening feels nourishing for you. Notice, too, how the other person responds.

Moments of well-being

7/11 breathing

When you feel that anxiety is building, stop what you are doing and focus on your breathing. Inhale for a comfortable count of 7 and exhale for a comfortable count of 11. If possible, inhale through the nostrils with mouth closed, and exhale through nostrils or mouth, whichever feels most natural for you. This has an immediate calming effect throughout the body and is similar to breathing into a paper bag when hyperventilating (although far less obvious!). Breathing in and out to this 7/11 ratio quickly corrects any blood gas imbalance and stimulates the body's relaxation response. Any physical discomfort, such as dizziness or tingling in the arms or legs, will then disappear.

Take some exercise

One of the fastest ways to shake off stress and relax is to exercise. Physical exertion quickly stimulates the release of endorphins (feel-good brain chemicals), which are natural pain-killers and create a sense of well-being.

Tune in: body, emotions, mind and spirit

From time to time, stop what you are doing. Close your eyes, turn your attention inwards and really notice how you are feeling on each dimension of well-being:

Physical: How does your body feel? Are you comfortable or is there some muscular tension, discomfort or tiredness?

Emotional: How are your emotions? Are you content, or are you feeling irritated, fed up, sad or demotivated?

Mental: How is your mind? Is it clear and focused, or are you finding it difficult to concentrate, thinking unhelpful thoughts, or buzzing with too much mental activity?

Spiritual: How are you spiritually? Are you feeling fulfilled and good about yourself, or do you feel isolated or disconnected?

Relax and breathe deeply for a few moments while you acknowledge your feelings. Then visualise yourself in the situation you were in a moment ago. Now, ask yourself what you can do that would make you feel better. Imagine making those adjustments, and then open your eyes.

Step back and observe yourself

When you are in any busy situation, step back mentally for a moment and observe what is happening. You are now viewing it from the outside, like watching a play in which you are one of the actors. This will give you a different, wider perspective on the situation and enable you to understand other people's responses. You can then notice what kind of role you are playing and ask yourself whether this is how you want to be.

Tool 2

Use your imagination

❝ I like to picture myself performing well in difficult situations. It gives me the confidence to do it for real! ❞

Our imagination is a uniquely human gift, and we can use it to improve our well-being. In our imagination, we can travel across space and time in an instant. We can revisit enjoyable events that have actually happened or conjure up scenes that inspire, relax or restore us.

We can also use this same resource to dwell on past, bad experiences or create future 'disasters', adversely affecting our health and well-being in the process. Focusing on what we don't want – the worst outcomes, the biggest obstacles – springs from underlying fear. In this state, we are unable to access our strengths and resources and act in our best interests. However, when we focus on how we want things to be, picturing ourselves handling situations well and doing what we really want in our lives, we are much more likely to meet with success. In fact, our imagination is like a virtual reality simulator that we can use to rehearse the success of any strategy we want to put in place. What we focus on we are more likely to achieve.

It can be really helpful to use our imagination in positive ways when we face challenges in our lives, whether we are sitting an exam, moving house or coping with the loss of a loved one. What we 'see' in our minds can help or hinder our capacity to cope, our self-confidence and our ability to counter our own and others' unhelpful actions. When we create scenes in which we are managing well, with all the supports around us that we need, we begin to feel stronger, safer and more in control. When the present is hard to bear, it can also help us if we imagine a better future.

We know that imagination has a powerful and immediate effect on our bodies. Just imagine biting into a lemon. You are probably salivating, even though you have not bitten into a lemon at all. Or recall an embarrassing scene: you may find yourself blushing! We can harness this in a positive way to improve our health and well-being. For example, clinical studies have shown that we can use our minds in this way to lower our blood pressure, lessen our experience of pain and even increase the number of certain types of immune cells in our bodies. Top sports people increase their speed and accuracy by imagining themselves going through their events and performing at their very best. Curiously, as they do so, it has been found that tiny electrical bursts of activity occur in the muscles they would use if they were doing it for real.

Imagining relaxing scenes can also benefit our emotional well-being. As our attention is directed away from our immediate circumstances, we find that tension and worry begin to melt away, and any anxiety and fears are replaced with feelings of deep rest and calm.

2

Using imagination as a positive tool in our lives is sometimes known as 'visualisation' or 'positive imagery'. It is not just about seeing pictures inside our heads. With practice, we can begin to use all our senses – sight, hearing, smell, touch and taste – and feeling – to create a positive vision of how we would like things to be. We can envisage how we would like to feel, think and act, and what we would like to achieve. As we do, we begin to reap the benefits of this practice for our overall well-being. At the same time, we can learn to change the negative images that may flow through our minds, images that can waste our energy, impair our physical health and impede our personal progress in life.

Benefits of using your imagination

Physical:

- improves our ability to relax deeply
- boosts our physical health and natural immunity

Emotional:

- increases our capacity to cope with difficult situations
- helps us to feel safe and in control

Mental:

- helps us to problem-solve more creatively and objectively
- enables us to rehearse success and develop new and different behaviours

Spiritual:

- enhances our self-esteem
- increases our sense of connection with something greater than ourselves, eg. nature, the universe or the Divine

2

Reflections

I had a really difficult meeting with my manager coming up. I practised visu-alising a successful encounter, where I looked calm and confident and could put forward my views in a logical and assertive way. When I floated into my body in that scene, I started to feel much calmer and I could get a sense of confidence flowing through my body and mind. I noticed how my manager was really listening to what I had to say and responding positively to me. It felt really good to feel I had some control in the situation, just by thinking and acting in a resourceful way. When the meeting finally happened, the fears I had had about the outcome just faded away. I handled myself well, I showed I could compromise and we came up with an unexpected solution.

I've been using my imagination to help me cope better with my chronic pain. I focus on what the pain looks, feels and sounds like – a heavy, dark grey block in my leg with hard edges that makes a dull, throbbing sound. Then I visualise it changing, growing lighter in weight and colour, becoming rounder, smoother and smaller, and the sound turning into music. Sometimes I see it floating away into the sky, like a balloon, until it is just a speck in a bright blue sky, which finally disappears. I then visualise being able to move more easily, even being able to run and dance again. I start to feel energised, invigorated and happier.

Sometimes I like to use my imagination as a means to get in touch with my own spirituality. I visualise myself sitting in a beautiful, still place and a light beginning to shine just inside my head, between my eyes. I imagine this light shining into my body and then out into the world, sending love to my family and friends, and then to all the people in the world who need comfort and healing. I also imagine the light going up into the universe, and connecting with a much bigger, brighter light. I get a sense of this light showering down on me, refreshing my mind, body and soul. I begin to feel a sensation of pure love for myself and for others. It helps me to stay balanced when things come along that, before, might have caused stress, upset or irritation.

2

How to practise using your imagination

 CD track

Use the following CD track to visualise and experience all the dimensions of well-being:

CD 1 Track 2: House of well-being (16¹/₂ mins)

Create your own visualisation

Visualisation can be focused on any or all of the dimensions of well-being, on particular strengths and qualities, or on the past or future, as the table below illustrates.

Visualisation

Dimension of well-being	Focus of visualisation
Physical	Achieving optimum health and vitality, stronger immune system, reduced pain, improved functioning (eg. digestion, mobility)
Emotional	Relaxation, reducing anxiety and other emotional arousal (eg. anger and irritation), strengthening motivation, self-confidence
Mental	Clear thinking, mental focus, problem solving
Spiritual	Sense of wonder, stillness, sanctuary, connection with others, the universe or the Divine
Resourcefulness	Handling difficult situations
Success	Performance in sport, music, public speaking, exams
The past	Past success or enjoyable times
The future	Preferred future

Each of us has a dominant sense; while some can see pictures quite vividly, others may hear sounds, feel textures, sense movement or even smell scents quite clearly in their imagination. As you begin to practise, you will develop more capacity to use all the senses.

2

Here are some simple steps to creating a positive visualisation:

1.   Decide on what you would like to achieve.

Have a look at the visualisation table on page 37, and also consider any specific needs you have. For example, you might choose:

-   a deep relax to offset the effects of a stressful day (emphasis on physical and emotional well-being)

-   a positive scene that builds your confidence and marshals your strengths for a forthcoming interview (emphasis on mental and emotional well-being).

2.   Relax.

It is important to get into a comfortable position so that your body does not distract you.

Use the tips for relaxation under 'Deep relax' on pages 28-29 to settle down ready for the next step.

3.   Create your scene.

Begin to use your imagination to shape images, feelings and sounds that are consistent with your intention. What are the feelings and sensations you would like to experience? For example, if you want to become a healthy, vibrant and happy person, what will you look like once you are that person? What will you be doing? What will you hear yourself saying? What colours will you be wearing? How will you feel?

Now ask yourself: 'What will my scene look like, feel like, sound like, smell like?' For example, if you want a deep rest, choose scenes that have a still quality, like lying on a beach where you can gaze at a calm, blue sky, feel the warmth of the sun on your skin and listen to the gentle sounds of waves lapping the shore. If you want to feel energised, create movement and energy in your scene, for example, walking or running beside a cascading river, feeling the wind in your face and hair, smelling the fresh scent of pine and hearing the calls of birds wheeling overhead. Nature is full of images, sounds and textures that you can incorporate into a scene for rest, inspiration, good energy or strength.

2

Take your time with this process, allowing images and sensations to arise spontaneously. You can then shape them in your mind's eye in terms of their colour, size, location, depth, brightness and volume, bringing in as much detail as you want.

4.   Absorb and enjoy.

Allow your attention to stay with your created scene. Distractions may arise from thoughts and parts of the scene coming and going, but these will lessen with practice. Just enjoy the images and sensations, absorbing the positive feelings they engender, rather than trying to control or analyse them.

As you relax, your intention, your desired scene and your absorption in it will all combine to bring about the intended improvements in your well-being.

Develop your vision of well-being

Practise your vision of optimum well-being that you developed at the beginning of this guide (see page 19) whenever you make time to relax. Embellish it with more and more detail so that it becomes familiar and easy to evoke. You may wish to draw on the CD track *House of well-being* to help you with this.

Later, you might also like to jot down what you have experienced. Alternatively, you could paint it, draw it or even write some poetry. This will deepen the experience and focus your mind on creating the reality.

Moments of well-being

Experiment with quick visualisations when you feel any sense of upset or disturbance. Just close your eyes, take three deep breaths in and out, and bring a positive scene into your mind for a few moments. Here are some examples:

Release negative feelings

If you feel angry, resentful, jealous etc, imagine gathering up these feelings and loading them into a basket attached to a large, brightly coloured air balloon tethered to the ground by a rope. If you are worried, picture yourself

2

writing your worries on sheets of paper and placing them in the basket. Get a sense of what it would be like to cut the rope and watch the balloon floating away in a blue sky, until it disappears. Feel the sun on your face and imagine you are laughing at the sky.

Recycle fear

If you begin to feel fearful, imagine stuffing that fear into a sack and tying up the opening securely. Imagine the effort of digging a large hole in the ground near the roots of a tree, then burying the sack deep in the earth. You can picture the fear decomposing and being taken up by the roots of the tree, so that it can be recycled in a positive way. Visualise a bright, colourful picture of yourself sitting under this flourishing tree, looking calm and happy. Sense other, helpful people alongside you if you feel you need extra support.

Get a guide

If you are facing a difficult situation, imagine that you have a guide or helper who can advise you on what to do. You might want to create a special place in your mind – a beautiful room or sheltered outdoor spot – where you can visit this guide. Your guide might be a special person, a spiritual energy or just a supportive, unseen presence. Imagine that you can share your thoughts and ask the questions you need answers to. Then notice any thoughts or feelings that come to you as you go about your day.

Heal the body

If you are ill, imagine what that illness looks like and where it is located in the body. You can give it a colour, shape, texture and even a sound, taste or smell. Then visualise a way of transforming it into something that feels like well-being for you – a new colour, shape, texture or other quality that gives you energy and a sense of wellness. Create this new image in as much detail as you can. Alternatively, you can imagine a coloured light or healing stream washing through the body, soothing away inflammation, pain or irritation, and strengthening healthy cells to overcome any foreign cells or infection.

Tool 3

Think positively

" I appreciate who I am and expect the best in my life "

What we think shapes the way we experience our life and well-being on all dimensions – physical, mental, emotional and spiritual. Learning to think positively increases our energy, while dwelling on negative thoughts drains it. Just as the body will benefit from a healthy, nutritious meal, feeding the mind with rich, positive thoughts boosts our resilience in all aspects of living.

An optimistic person looks at a half-filled glass of water as half 'full', while a pessimistic person judges it to be half 'empty'. An optimist interprets difficult times as temporary, specific to one situation and unconnected to any shortcomings of their own, while the pessimist believes that their troubles will last forever, affect everything they do and are caused by failures in themselves. The pessimist will even put a 'negative spin' on a good event, believing it to be unconnected to their own strengths and actions, and unlikely to last for very long or have any positive effect on the rest of their lives. Even in the face of success they may still give up, interpreting any personal achievement as just a 'fluke'.

This tendency towards a sense of helplessness means that pessimists have been shown to be much more likely to experience poorer physical health, shorter lives and rockier relationships than optimists. In contrast, optimists are happier, are more resistant to disease and enjoy life more.

Learning to think positively puts us in touch with our own creativity and strengths in the face of any challenge, enabling us to bounce back from our troubles. It also helps us to believe that the good things that happen to us will be lasting; when we succeed, we 'get on a roll' and are able to withstand pressure, rather than collapse under it. Above all, believing that good events will enhance everything we do provides the bedrock of hope.

So how can we develop positive thinking and hope? Negative thinking is an unconscious habit, just like biting our nails or watching too much TV. The first step is to learn to notice and observe our thoughts. Becoming the observer requires us to be relaxed, so that we can take a step back from our own internal thinking and what is happening around us (see *Relax and tune in* on page 21). We can then check whether our thoughts are mainly positive or negative.

The next step is to start challenging the thoughts that are not helpful to us – thoughts like, 'I'm hopeless at...', for example, or 'I could never do that' or 'Everything's ruined'. If someone we valued said to us, 'I'm a complete

3

failure', we would not let them get away with such hopeless thinking. We would try our hardest to dispute such a negative statement by coming up with a whole list of reasons and evidence that this was just not accurate. But how often do we dispute our own thoughts? Just because *we* think them, we tend to believe they are completely true! Most difficult events have many causes, but we may latch on to the one that lasts longest and affects the biggest part of our lives. So next time you notice yourself having an unhelpful thought, imagine you are in a courtroom and you are prosecuting your own unhelpful thoughts and beliefs.

Once we have challenged our thoughts, we can begin to change them into more resourceful ones. On page 45 you will find an exercise called 'HOPE', which will help you to begin to change any negative or destructive thinking. We can also steer ourselves away from negative thinking by distracting ourselves with an activity we enjoy and that absorbs us.

Even when we cannot change a situation or influence the way others respond, we always have the power to change the way we think. Since thoughts can be the seeds of beliefs, attitudes, feelings, speech and actions, this can have enormous benefits for our well-being. Taking responsibility for changing our thoughts helps us to feel less anxious, more in control and helpfully detached from the emotions of others. Creating and sustaining positive thoughts is like exercising a muscle – the more we do it, the stronger those 'thought fibres' or neural connections become.

We can train ourselves to respond to difficult situations and challenges by thinking and feeling positively. We can do this by remembering times when things did go well or we did cope, as well as visualising future success (see *Use your imagination* on page 33). You will discover that practising in this way strengthens a positive cycle of thinking and that successful outcomes tend to happen. The old habit of 'doom and gloom' thinking changes to one of hope and enthusiasm.

Learning to think positively is one of the foundation stones of well-being. As we practise, we become more appreciative. We value ourselves, what we do, our surroundings and other people more. We begin to look at what has gone well, rather than at our failures and mistakes. We see the goodness in life. Appreciation may then become the basis for spiritual practice, where we give thanks to something greater than ourselves for guiding and sustaining us.

3

Benefits of thinking positively

Physical:

- promotes good health and longevity

- increases energy and aids recovery from illness

Emotional:

- increases hopefulness and appreciation

- reduces worrying and boosts ability to tolerate uncertainty

Mental:

- improves ability to understand and change our thoughts in helpful ways

- makes tasks seem easier

Spiritual:

- fosters self-understanding and closer connections with others

- helps to provide a sense of meaning and contentment in life

Reflections

*I was stuck in negative thinking after my father died. I felt depressed and just couldn't see the point in anything. I dwelt on the things I hadn't done with him when he was alive. Then a friend gently challenged me into listing everything I **had** done. There were many happy times I remembered, as well as the support I had given him during his illness. She then pointed out my positive qualities. As a result, I began to feel I could use these not only to help myself but in my work. I now feel much more hopeful about life.*

When our house got flooded, it seemed like the last straw. So many things had gone wrong and I began to believe that nothing would ever get better. It wasn't until I had a couple of days away that I began to see the kind of

3

thinking pattern I had got myself into. I work in IT and, given that the brain is like a computer, I knew that I could reprogram my thoughts. So every time I caught myself thinking negatively, I said to myself, 'Delete that program!' I then deliberately thought something more helpful as if I were setting up a new program. As I think more positively, those new programs are easier to 'run' and the connections between external events and positive thoughts seem to get stronger.

I use positive affirmations to help me cope with my illness. I say things like, 'Every day my body is getting stronger' and 'I have all the energy I need'. I say them with conviction and enthusiasm several times a day and even pin them on my fridge door! Somehow it helps to put them in the present tense, as if I have already achieved them, I feel I am sowing the seeds of better health and well-being at a deep level. Although it's very simple, it really seems to help me feel a lot better and make real progress.

How to practise thinking positively

 CD track

This track will help you experience a way of changing unhelpful thoughts into positive and resourceful ones, just as if you were directing your own film.

CD 1 Track 3: Film director (11 mins)

HOPE

Here is a simple way of creating more hopeful thoughts. Look at the example below and then follow the steps of **HOPE** yourself and notice the difference it makes.

Example

Something 'bad' happens (or you imagine something bad happening), like an exam proving more difficult than you had expected.

You react with an unhelpful thought:

3

'I'm a total failure. I'm never going to get the job I set my heart on.'

Left unchecked, this thought may lead to an immediate loss of energy and motivation, as you begin to feel sad and helpless. More unhelpful thoughts follow, for example:

'I can't even muster the energy to work for the next exam. What's the point?'

Instead of getting into this negative cycle of thinking, you can follow the HOPE steps *as soon as you begin to have the first unhelpful thought.*

H – Hold everything! Just stop that thought and concentrate on relaxing.

O – Observe. When you relax, your emotions calm down and you begin to see things in perspective. Why is this thought so unhelpful? What would you say if your best friend voiced this thought? What can you learn about yourself from this initial reaction, eg. the beliefs you have about yourself and life? By observing, you can begin to look at this difficulty for what it is. For example, just how important or serious is it in the scheme of things?

P – Possibilities. With a wider perspective, feeling relaxed, you can now begin to generate possibilities – new ways of thinking and reacting, which you might not have considered before. For example:

'Most people found the exam difficult. The grades will reflect that and I may do better than I hoped.'

'Even if I don't get the grade, I can resit the paper or bring my overall grade up by working hard for the next exams.'

'I don't need to get the very best grade to get that job. I have a lot of relevant experience and that is going to count for a lot.'

E – Energy. You feel an increase in energy and motivation to overcome this difficulty or obstacle. You can then have further helpful and hopeful thoughts:

*'Right, I'm going to really put some effort into revising for the next exams. I **can** do it, I've done it before and I can do it now!'*

3

Appreciation audit

We often look at the things that went wrong and talk about 'learning from our mistakes'. But how often do we take time to learn and grow from an appreciation of what went right?

Reflect on a recent situation that went well:

- What worked well?
- What did you contribute?
- What did others contribute?

Reflect on a situation you are in, where things are currently difficult. Instead of wondering who is at fault or why this is happening to you, consider the following:

- What is working well here?
- What have I done well already?
- What have others done well already?
- What alternatives do I still have?
- How can I best work with others to find a solution?

3

Moments of well-being

Watch your language

Notice the sort of words you use to describe your experiences. If you use negative terms, turn them into more positive statements that make you feel better, as the examples below demonstrate:

Negative	Positive
It's a problem.	It's a challenge.
I'm freezing.	It could be warmer.
My teenage daughter is a nightmare.	I remember what it's like to be a teenager.
I'm so tired.	It's going to feel so good when I get into bed.
I have a cold and feel terrible.	This is a good reason to give myself a treat.
The weather is awful.	The garden could really do with this rain.

The last three examples in the list show how we can look for opportunity and benefit in any situation and focus on that.

STOP!

Sometimes, your thoughts can cause havoc with your emotions. At these times, it is useful to think, 'STOP!'. Here, the word is used like a full-stop at the end of a sentence. It replaces or stalls any further thought and encourages you to cease dwelling, speaking or acting on it. You can then distract yourself by doing something that absorbs you.

Be grateful

Each morning, before you get up or at the start of your day, spend a minute appreciating the day ahead. Make a mental note of three things you can look forward to, perhaps meeting a friend, having some free time or sorting out a task that has been on your mind. Notice how this makes you feel inside and how energy begins to flow towards these things.

3

Spend a minute at the end of each day mentally listing three things you are grateful for, such as the sun shining, getting to the gym, a visit from a friend or finishing a piece of work. If you wish, you can note these down and begin to create a journal of positive thoughts. Remember to give some thanks to yourself too! Notice how this appreciation makes you feel inside.

Spend any minute you can in nature, appreciating its beauty. Feel the textures, breathe in the scents, feast your eyes on the colours and shapes and revitalise your whole system.

Stick to positive people

Think of some of the people you know – friends, relatives, colleagues or just acquaintances. When you are with them, which ones make you feel good? They are usually the ones who are more positive about life and ready to compliment you and others. You can choose to spend more time with them. Not only will it make you feel better, but you can learn from them.

Praise yourself

When you do something well, praise yourself. If someone else recognises what you have done or thanks you for it, really take that on board. Stop and breathe it in, and later think back on how good that felt. Even without thanks, you can think positively about your achievements and your special attributes.

Tool 4

Be creative

When I am being creative,
I feel truly alive

Being creative fills us with energy and enthusiasm, and lifts our well-being. To feel inspired is to feel content and fulfilled. Being creative is about getting in touch with a unique human attribute. It is a way of expressing our relationship with the world, and giving voice to our feelings and experience.

While the left side of the brain handles logic, lists, words, numbers and rational analysis, the right side is concerned with very different activities: daydreaming, imagination, images, rhythm, colour, music and spatial awareness. Einstein once said that 'imagination is more important than knowledge'. Like many other great scientists, he would deliberately spend time 'daydreaming' to engage the powers of the creative side of the brain. Einstein was not at his desk or working on a blackboard when he came up with the theory of relativity; he was relaxing on a hillside in the sunshine, imagining sitting on a sunbeam!

When we engage the immense resource of our imagination, we often experience a feeling that time is standing still. Our thoughts slow down, awareness of activity and noise around us fades out and we seem to reach a quiet, inner space full of potential. From this place, we can generate new ways of seeing things and wonderful new futures; we can express our experience and connect with our unique selves at a deeper level.

Giving 'voice' to our creativity is essentially healing on all levels and has been recognised as such by the introduction of art therapies in healthcare. Just like scientific enquiry, the creative arts provide us with a means of harnessing our imagination and creativity in order to explore ourselves and how we relate to the world. Unlike science, however, they thrive on our capacity to see the humorous, the absurd, the beautiful and the ambiguous in our experience. Spending time in creative pursuits like painting, writing, music or dancing provides us with the time and space to allow the unexpected to emerge.

Many of us say that we are not creative, perhaps remembering the childlike drawings or paintings we produced long ago. However, when we think about creativity as a *process*, we can enjoy and immerse ourselves in the *doing*, rather than be concerned about what we produce at the end. In fact, everything we do in day-to-day living can be done differently and more creatively. Once we are fully engaged in the creative process, we can soar above the constraints of our situation and surprise ourselves with new ways of seeing things. This can make us feel revitalised, more energetic and fulfilled.

4

Bringing creativity into our lives provides us with a way to generate new solutions and ideas. Rarely does a big idea come into our heads as a complete package in an instant. While they might seem like gifts that arrive from somewhere outside ourselves, or 'Eureka!' moments, creative ideas are often the product of working on problems over a longer period of time. This work goes on at a 'deeper' level than conscious thinking. Elements of ideas come when we give them space to appear and a chance to develop. This is why having quiet times helps to still the mind and allows ideas to emerge (see *Discover peace* on page 77). Equally, when we are totally taken up with something else, a solution to a problem may appear.

By learning to relax and unleash the capacity of the right-hand brain, we can increase our thinking potential on all fronts. We can use this potential for our own personal growth. We can also achieve peak performance in our work, in music, in sport or indeed in any activity. When we reach this state, we feel that we are 'in flow' or 'in the zone'. Time stands still and we perform at our very best, without having any conscious thoughts about what we are doing and how we are doing it.

Working with others towards a common goal can also be a highly creative process, if we pay attention to the conditions. When we are in a group working together, we need to set aside normal roles and a sense of pre-judging. We can then bounce ideas off each other and the group seems to produce results above and beyond the capacities of the individuals involved.

When we allow fear and anxiety to dominate our thinking, we greatly restrict the solutions and choices we are able to see and can fall into a pattern of 'black and white' thinking. We dwell on the obstacles and 'cannot see the wood for the trees'. When we lose the wider perspective we also lose the ability to create a range of possibilities for action. On the other hand, we can foster 'possibility thinking' through learning to relax deeply (see *Relax and tune in* on page 21). As we set aside current concerns and allow the busy, anxious mind to calm down, we can 'take a step back' and see the bigger picture, detached from the urgency of our emotions. We can create new perspectives and options we may not have seen or noticed before. These are often more flexible and robust solutions than those we might have had to settle for.

4

Benefits of being creative

Physical:

- recharges our energy
- reduces physical tension and the experience of pain

Emotional:

- provides a route to exploring and expressing our feelings
- increases our capacity to stay calm and resourceful

Mental:

- avoids 'over-thinking' and dwelling on problems
- helps us to generate new ideas and solutions

Spiritual:

- allows us to express ourselves in our own, unique ways
- increases self-knowledge and appreciation
- bypasses the busy, thinking mind and enables us to find a still place within

Reflections

When I retired, I decided to take up art and I went back to college. It was something I had always wanted to do and never had the time for, as I had to commute every day to work. I started off feeling very tentative and wondered whether I was just too old to take the course. Over time, I was encouraged to explore, be experimental and really push beyond my limits. I now produce huge pieces of abstract art which amaze me, as well as my family and friends! I have had a small exhibition and art has become a vital part of my life.

4

> *When I'm searching for a work solution, I've learned to relax and let my mind just drift. I stimulate the process by jotting down some key thoughts on a page, either as words or pictures or both. I often do this before I go to sleep so I can weave them into my dreams. It's incredible how ideas pop up out of the blue – never when I'm actively thinking about the problem!*

> *My kids were bored, so I got out some of my old magazines, some glue and glitter. As they started to get busy, I grabbed a sheet of paper and joined in. I had the notion of creating something that would make me feel good when I looked at it. I quickly found images that appealed to me – roses, a water-fall, smiling faces, a sunset, mountains – and organised them onto the page. I was so absorbed that I carried on, even though the children had finished and gone to watch TV. The resulting picture really surprised me – it did make me feel good! I put it up in my bedroom and I look at it before I go to sleep and when I wake up.*

How to practise being creative

 CD track

Experience the feelings of expressing yourself creatively and stimulate your problem-solving capacity by listening to the following track:

CD 2 Track 1: Creative garden (11^1/$_2$ mins)

A picture of well-being

One form of creative artwork is collage. This only requires a collection of old magazines, scissors and glue, although you can add other materials if you wish, such as photographs, pieces of fabric, glitter, paints etc. This is some-thing you can enjoy doing alone or with a group of friends.

Set aside an hour and have some fun creating a picture of well-being for you. What does your perfect well-being look like? If you allow yourself to relax and just go with the process, you will begin to find images, words, shapes and textures that you want to incorporate into the overall picture, even though you may not know why.

4

When you have finished, look at what you have created: something uniquely 'you'. Suspend any judgment of your picture as a work of art. How do you feel when you look at it? Does it uplift or inspire you? If so, you may wish to put it up somewhere you can see it in your day-to-day life.

Creative mind maps

This is a powerful way of generating ideas and organising your thoughts around a problem, project or idea.

Take a sheet of paper and in the centre draw an image of the topic or problem around which you wish to generate your creative ideas. Working quickly, branch off from the centre, writing down ideas and connecting them wherever they seem to fit in, as fast as they come into your head.

Keep each new idea as a single word on its own line, because a single word will spark off more ideas and images than it will do if it is buried in a sentence. Images and words on the branches near the centre will usually be the primary ideas. Secondary ideas will branch out towards the boundary of the page. Look out for the same idea or image popping up all over the place, however, because this may be the underlying concept, which will form the heart of your problem-solving or exploration.

When you have finished, you can create further clarity and associations by adding different colours, underlining or outlining, to highlight relationships within your mind map.

Rearrange your room

Next time you go into your living room, bedroom or office, stop for a minute and look around. Is there something in the room that could be rearranged to make the room feel better? Rearranging the furniture, pictures or other objects, taking something out or putting something in can all help to improve your feeling of well-being when you spend time there.

4

Moments of well-being

Creative moments

Make a quick, spontaneous list of small, creative things you could do, for example:

- buy a bunch of flowers for yourself and arrange them

- collect inspiring poems or quotes

- decorate a cake or card for a friend

- listen to some beautiful music and use it to create pictures in your mind

- plan an uplifting new colour scheme for a room.

Set aside some time to do something on your list and notice how you feel while you are doing it.

Creative solutions

This is a way of exercising your mind to find creative solutions to problems.

Imagine you are writing a script for a cartoon and one of the characters has fallen off a cliff. Think of as many ways as possible for the character to escape from the situation – anything is possible in cartoons!

Doodle

Find a large piece of paper and some coloured pens or paints and spend a few minutes filling the page with colour or design. It does not have to represent anything. This is more about just doing something creative rather than trying to achieve a result.

4

Write poetry

Think of a special, happy experience you have had. Now, as quickly as you can, write down on a blank piece of paper every thought in your head relating to that experience. When you have spent a few moments doing that, re-read what you have written and underline any phrases that seem poetic. Write them down on a separate piece of paper and that is your poem.

Capture ideas

Ideas often pop into our heads and equally quickly pop out again. So when one does appear, write it down. Carry a small booklet with you and put it by your bedside table at night to capture good ideas, which often come as we begin to wake up.

Change your look

Think about what you normally wear and try something different. Try a different colour, a new style or haircut.

Cook up something new

Change your usual recipes, buy some different or unusual ingredients and enjoy cooking something new.

Messy play

Ever played with making mud balls, sculpting clay, or shaping plasticine or playdough? It is messy but great fun. It really gives a sense of moulding and creating something solid.

Daydream

Make some time each day to allow your thoughts to wander. There will always be gaps when you are waiting for someone or you are between tasks.

Tool 5

Lighten up

"When I laugh, everything seems easier"

Learning to see the lighter side in any situation by allowing play and laughter into our lives lifts our own mood as well as the mood of those around us. 'Lightening up' in this way is infectious and spreads happiness. If we let our inner joyful nature shine through, we will reap many benefits for our well-being.

Life can be a serious business when we feel beset with difficulties and problems. We can find ourselves in a dark place where it is difficult to imagine that there is a lighter side. Those around us can compound our anxiety or despair with their own negative thoughts and feelings. However, we can learn to be 'play-full' in the way we engage with life, even during challenging times. This can help us to let go of barriers and overcome difficulties.

As the famous Shakespeare quote goes, *'All the world's a stage, And all the men and women merely players.'* We play many roles in the course of our lives but we all have a choice in terms of *how* we play them and how we respond to the drama of life. Playful people are like the 'wise fool', having an easiness with both success and failure in themselves and others. We all have a playful side and when we find it we experience a wonderful feeling of liberation. It brings a 'lightness' into the proceedings, which encourages tolerance in our listening and softness in our judgments. It helps to create a balance between maintaining self-respect and having an easy way with others.

When we watch children play, they seem to be totally caught up in the moment, unaware of how they look to the outside world. In contrast, we usually picture adults playing organised sports or games, where there are many rules and norms of behaviour. As adults, we rarely consider playing for playing's sake. In fact, we may feel that it is childish or indulgent to just 'play'. We feel embarrassed at the very thought of making fools of ourselves in front of other people. Yet it is play that allows us to drop the roles and masks we wear and bring more of who we truly are to the fore. As we detach from the 'ego', a natural easiness becomes apparent. We participate to the full and this can be a moving experience.

With play, goals become unimportant as long as we are doing something we enjoy. The important thing is to allow ourselves to be spontaneous and carefree, willing to take the risk of getting it wrong. Playing with others, whether through organised games, making music, dancing or just having fun, has an important social dimension. It encourages a quality of interaction that can be more fulfilling than our normal conversations and

5

contacts. It creates a deeper sense of connection, beyond our words and actions.

Laughter, too, boosts our sense of well-being. Laughing with ourselves and others helps us to keep a balanced perspective and learn from our behaviour. It enhances self-esteem and enables us to connect with others at a deeper level. Laughter has proven physical and mental benefits, including boosting the immune system, improving sleep, enhancing mental function and increasing pain tolerance. Laughter releases endorphins (feel-good brain chemicals) around our bodies. Even remembering a time when you laughed long and hard, or going through the motions of smiling and laughing can trigger these effects. It is no wonder that clowns are now being introduced onto some hospital wards.

We can also bring light into our lives by creating opportunities for celebration. Many of our traditional celebrations, linked as they were to religion or working the land, have fallen away. These were times when people dressed up, danced, made music, laughed and played. Although weddings, festivals and parties continue to provide opportunities for light-hearted connection, we don't need a big occasion to provide a reason for celebration. With a little awareness, we can celebrate the good moments of life and living in many ways, either alone or with others. We can light a candle, hug someone or give flowers as spontaneous celebrations of life's small, special moments. We can create our own traditions of celebration that bring loved ones, social groups, local communities and even work teams together to enjoy each other's company and to play.

Benefits of lightening up

Physical:

- releases tension and reduces stress
- provides many health benefits

Emotional:

- diffuses anger and negative emotions
- promotes better communication with others

Mental:

- helps us to put things in perspective and see the 'lighter' side

- helps us to overcome barriers and difficulties

Spiritual:

- enables self-expression and self-learning

- promotes an atmosphere of mutual respect and community with others

Reflections

"I sometimes go away for a short walking break with my girlfriends. As we stroll along, we seem to spend most of the time laughing about all kinds of things, and sometimes about nothing at all! Something silly can spark us off and we laugh until we cry. It makes me feel very close to my friends and puts my worries into perspective."

"I have always loved to create special times of celebration for my family, whether around festive times, individual achievements or 'comings and goings'. But I've come to discover that it's the small rituals that seem to provide the 'glue' in our lives – sending a goodnight text to each other when we are apart, having a group hug when there's reason for happiness or sadness, hanging up bunches of balloons for everyone's birthdays, however old they are."

"I play golf with my mates. It means a lot to me – not to win the game but to be part of the group, sharing a joke and laughing at myself when a shot goes wrong. It's good to get out in the fresh air and enjoy the views, but it's the fun we have that I really enjoy and makes me feel good. All the tension of the week just slips away."

5

How to practise lightening up

 ## CD track

Recall and re-experience the lightness and spontaneity of playing as a child with the following track:

CD 2 Track 2: Snow play (9¹/₂ mins)

Play and enjoyment audit

1. Make some notes in response to the following questions and then take some of the ideas this generates into each day:

When did you last have a good laugh?

- What sparked it off?
- How did you respond? How did you feel?
- How did others respond?

When did you last do something spontaneous and playful?

- What sparked it off?
- How did you respond? How did you feel?
- How did others respond?

When did you last celebrate something in your life?

- What did you do?
- How did it feel?
- How did others respond?

2. What do you do to play?

3. Rate your current level of playfulness in life from 0 (low) to 10 (high). What could you do to increase your rating by 1 point?

5

Celebrate

Create a celebration around something you might normally let slip by, for example, recovery from an illness, a work achievement, the arrival of summer. It could be something you celebrate alone or something you wish to involve other, significant people in. Make it special with music, activity, dress, food or surroundings. Invite others to contribute in their own ways.

Enjoy a funny film

Go and see a comedy play or film. Collect your favourite comedy films and watch one of them if you are feeling low.

Moments of well-being

Smile

When you are relaxing or have just woken up in the morning, imagine smiling into your body. Smile into your lungs, your heart and each organ, thanking them for doing such a good job. You can then smile into your bones, your muscles, your blood and so on. Imagine each part of your body smiling back.

Smile at yourself with your eyes closed, imagining the smile lighting up your face and eyes, then open your eyes and smile at yourself in the mirror.

Smile at other people and notice their reactions. They will nearly always smile back. Smiling, like laughter, is infectious and makes you and others feel good too.

Laugh

Laughing is good for you, so even when there is nothing to laugh about, try having a laugh anyway. Take a deep breath in and let it go by laughing out loud. Do this several times. Going through the motions of laughing has all the same benefits as laughing 'for real' and you may find that one leads to the other.

Remember a time when you laughed until you cried or your sides ached. If you can't remember a time, imagine what it would be like to laugh helplessly, and allow the feeling to rise up inside you.

Even if you are not good at telling jokes, if you hear a good one write it down. Keep it for yourself or share it with friends in person or on the internet.

Do something different

Do something spontaneous and playful and see how it feels.

Now think of something playful you wish you had done; decide to take a risk and do it. The worst that could happen is that you will look silly. The best is that you will discover how easy and good it feels to have fun. So go for it!

Dance

Collect your top ten songs that have a dance rhythm. Play them when your well-being score drops. If you are self-conscious, choose a time when you are on your own; otherwise, have a party. Listen to the music and the rhythm and let your body move to the sounds.

Play with your children

Next time your small children or grandchildren are playing, join in, not as an adult instructing them but to co-operate with their game. Learn from them. They love to have fun and live in the moment.

Be easy on yourself

We are our own worst critics. Holding onto shame or guilt is harmful for our well-being. Try not to judge yourself, and learn to let go of mistakes. Forgiving yourself enables you to move on and will definitely lighten your load.

5

Tool 6

Value yourself

❝When I nurture myself, I begin to grow in confidence and self-respect ❞

How we view ourselves, how we describe ourselves and how we look after ourselves are central to our feeling of well-being. This lays the foundation for recovery, self-discovery and positive change.

Self-care is not just about looking after our physical body, although giving ourselves wholesome food, sufficient sleep and regular exercise is an important component. It is about giving ourselves a chance to renew and heal on all levels – physical, mental, emotional and spiritual. Making time for self-nurturing fosters our self-esteem and self-respect. Self-esteem comes from valuing ourselves and recognising what makes us special. When we begin to recognise our own worth, we can see the goodness in others. This builds mutual respect and improves our relationships. Showing self-respect also provides an example to others and encourages them to take more care of themselves.

Very often, when we are busy or worried about others, it is easy to forget about caring for ourselves. It may be that we think others should come first and that we are somehow less important. However, just like the advice from aircrew to put our oxygen masks on first before we help other people with theirs, we need to take care of ourselves before we are able to look after anyone else. If we do not attend to our own human needs, we risk burn-out – where we become physically and emotionally exhausted and have nothing left to give (see *Meet your needs* on page 27).

One of the biggest hurdles to valuing ourselves can be the regular personal 'put-downs' we say to ourselves, for example, 'I am not good enough' or 'I got that wrong again'. It is all too easy to ignore our own achievements and contributions and develop a negative self-image. However, we can start to change this by learning to appreciate the good things about ourselves and to praise ourselves for things we have done well. We can remember times when we have really done our best or when we have said something to encourage others.

We are often busy caring for others but how often do we allow ourselves to be cared for? Other people like to be helpful but sometimes it can be hard for us to accept help graciously. We may even find it difficult to accept a compliment. Opening ourselves to another's care, whether on a physical level such as a massage, or on an emotional-spiritual level when we unburden our troubles, can be a gift to them as well as to ourselves.

When we are faced with difficult circumstances, emotional trauma or suffering, it is important to know who to turn to for support. Recognising that we do need someone to share our thoughts and feelings with is an important part of self-care and confidence. At work, this may be a colleague, mentor or line manager. In our personal lives, it may be a partner or close friend. Sometimes, we may need the services of a professional therapist or counsellor.

One of the biggest challenges for our self-care is change, particularly when it is imposed on us by someone else, such as our managers or the government. If we have not been consulted or involved in the decision-making, we can be left feeling powerless. However, one thing we do have control over is our own thinking and this, in turn, determines our attitude and behaviour (see *Think positively* on page 41). We can then begin to see that there are many aspects of our life in which we can exercise some control and make changes that improve our level of well-being. An important first step we can take is deciding what we want for ourselves and making time to reflect on it. We can use our imagination to create a rich, compelling vision of how we would like things to be, on a personal, social and environmental level (see *Use your imagination* on page 33).

When we do bring new things into our life to improve our well-being, we need to create space for them. This may involve letting go. Just as we throw out old clothes and shoes to make space in our wardrobe for new outfits, we can release feelings of guilt about what we 'ought' to do or 'should' have done. We can forgive ourselves and others for past mistakes, which allows us to let go of the negative emotions still attached to our memories.

Every day we seek pleasure, often through things outside ourselves, such as our possessions, our relationships, satisfying our physical needs or trying to fulfil our ambitions for status and wealth. We get attached to the things we think we 'own' and driven by the desire for yet more. Eventually, we may discover that this leaves us short of lasting happiness. However, we all have inner resources – our own values and qualities – that can foster contentment. It is when we recognise these and put them to use in our lives that we start to feel satisfied and content, and our well-being improves on all levels. Values such as love, courage, honesty, wisdom and compassion are important guiding beliefs that we all have. We can develop them through practice and begin to experience a feeling of balance and wholeness. We come to understand and accept ourselves at a deep level for who we are and, at the same time, we can review and change beliefs and attitudes that prove to be unhelpful. We can draw on our inner understanding to develop a confidence that is based on self-respect and humility, rather than on arrogance or power over others.

It is the turning inwards and recognising the riches of our own spiritual values that leads us towards true happiness. It gives us the inner strength to live and act by being true to ourselves, regardless of what is happening around us. It is not an easy path to follow, as we are held back by our own attitudes and habits, as well as being influenced by the negative beliefs and attitudes of others. By constantly reminding ourselves that we are peaceful beings with all the wisdom we need within, we can begin to feel a more real and lasting sense of happiness (see *Discover peace* on page 77). By first making changes in ourselves, we can also make a contribution to creating a better world.

Benefits of valuing yourself

Physical:

⊛ encourages us to take care of our physical health and well-being

Emotional:

⊛ alerts us to meet our emotional needs in healthy and satisfying ways

⊛ helps us to identify the supports we need around us

Mental:

⊛ recognises our own achievements and contributions

⊛ helps us to know when we need to turn to others for support

Spiritual:

⊛ enables us to recognise our inner strengths and improve our self-esteem

⊛ gets us in touch with our spiritual values as the basis for fulfilment and lasting happiness

6

Reflections

I spent a lot of years being angry with my brother because of things that happened a long time ago. I began to realise how it was damaging my own well-being and causing unnecessary suffering to others. When I thought about the past, I recognised that he was probably just doing the best he could do at that time and hadn't intended to hurt me. I sent him an email and asked if we could meet up. It was so good to make contact again. We acknowledged the importance of our relationship and it wasn't long before we were enjoying doing all kinds of things together. I feel I have released a burden and am much lighter in myself.

When I lost my wife, I had lots of offers of help from people but I kept telling them I was alright, as I had always been very capable and had looked after myself and her. It took a bad fall to make me realise that it isn't a failing to ask for help and that it also makes the other person feel good. Now I do ask my family and friends for assistance when I need it and sometimes, even when I don't! With a bit of support I can start to enjoy life again and deepen my relationships with the people who are still in my life.

I used to juggle work, kids and social life and never find time for myself. When I got ill, it was a bit of a wake-up call. I'm recovering now, but I make sure I eat well, make time for rest and exercise, and most important of all, give myself some treats without feeling guilty. I have even spent quiet moments thinking about what makes me a special person. I have then realised that people value me for who I am, rather than all the things I do. It helps me to let go of doing things which just aren't important.

How to practise valuing yourself

 CD track

Experience what it is like to rediscover what makes you special by listening to the following track:

CD 2 Track 3: Hidden treasures (10$^1/_2$ mins)

6

Values audit

From the list below, give yourself a score from 0 to 10 for each value. The top scores are your strengths, the lower ones are those you need to develop:

Value	Score
Patience	
Generosity	
Calmness	
Enthusiasm	
Kindness	
Humour	
Consideration	
Honesty	
Efficiency	
Tolerance	
Courage	

My strengths

Look at your top three values from the values audit.

- Which of these values would you like to develop even more?

Think of a time when you felt inspired, empowered, engaged and fully 'you'.

- What personal values do you now see were in operation at that time?

- What other strengths and qualities do you see in yourself?

Experience personal values

Relax your body using the relaxation practice on page 29. In your mind, allow an image or feeling of your deepest, inner values to arise. Focus on one value. Does a shape, colour, sound or phrase come to mind, associated with that value? Take time to really experience it. What is it like to be that value? Choose another value, and experience it as deeply as you can in the same way. In your own time, move on to a third value. Now remember these three values, experiencing each in turn. Then gradually become more aware of your body and your surroundings and open your eyes.

Look for support

When you have felt supported by someone in a difficult situation, what are the qualities or values that they have shown towards you? In turn, when you have helped someone during a tough time, what personal strengths and values did you draw on?

Making a list of people you would choose to turn to for support in different circumstances helps you to identify the qualities you look for in others during times of trouble. Who would you turn to in each of the following situations:

- losing your house keys
- making a mistake at work
- having had an argument with a friend
- needing a chat when you are feeling low
- experiencing a death in the family
- being diagnosed with a serious illness.

Self-care plan

In the grid on page 74, list all the ways you currently take care of yourself in the first row in each column – physical, emotional, mental and spiritual. You may find that some things contribute to well-being on more than one dimension.

Complete the rest of the grid in the same way, coming up with ideas for improving your self-care and identifying the supports you will need to do this.

	Physical	Emotional	Mental	Spiritual
Things I currently do	*eg. go for a run each day*			
Things I will do	*eg. eat breakfast before I go to work*			
Special treats I will have	*eg. a lie-in with the papers on Sundays*			
Things I will let go of	*eg. smoking*			
Support I will need to make the changes	*eg. smoking cessation clinic, partners consent to the (joint) lie-in!*			

Moments of well-being

Ask for and give help

Many of us find it difficult to ask for help, which is curious because most people like to be helpful. The act of looking after someone or something enhances our well-being. So learn to ask for help when you feel you need it, and to offer help when you feel you can give it. It only takes an instant – but the benefits for both parties are well worthwhile.

Nurturing steps

When you are out walking or running, get a sense of the rhythm in your steps and repeat some personal strengths you would like to develop in time to your movement, words like 'peace', 'calm', 'clarity' and 'joy'. This helps you to focus on your own positive qualities and gives an uplifting sense of being in control. Even a short walk along a corridor or pathway reciting qualities in time with your step will be sufficient to nurture the spirit.

The golden sphere

If you are worried about someone else, or you are fearful for yourself, conjure up a golden sphere or ball of light in your imagination and place an image of that person or yourself inside it. This sphere can represent the energy of light and goodness. You might imagine it connecting not only with your inner source of power but with a universal source of peace and love. Try it and see how it works.

Reflect on your values

At the end of the day, spend a minute reflecting on how you have used your strengths and values that day. How does this make you feel? Thank yourself before going to sleep.

Treat yourself

Treat yourself to something special. Do something that you enjoy. It is important that you look after yourself, especially if you are having to look after others.

Let go

There are many things that we do out of habit or because we feel we ought to. Think of something that you do not really like doing and consider what would happen if you stopped doing it. There may be creative ways to find a solution. Remember to imagine how it would feel if you never had to do it again!

6

Tool 7

Discover peace

> *" When I tap into the silence inside myself, I feel I can handle anything "*

There are times alone when we can enjoy our own company and get a sense of what it is like to be peaceful. It may be when we are relaxing in a bath or watching nature's beauty. Sometimes we may wake up in the morning just feeling good about life and grateful to be alive. At other times, it may be listening to inspiring music or watching a sleeping baby that gives us that feeling of balance and contentment. These moments provide a glimpse of our natural, peaceful state that too often is elusive and transitory. Peacefulness is a quality we all have but have forgotten. The following section looks at how, with conscious understanding and practice, we can begin to become more 'ourselves' and experience the benefits of peace.

Finding a time for silence gives us an opportunity to discover our inner peace. It enhances our well-being at all levels, and instils a sense of stability when everything around us may be in turmoil. The practice of stilling the mind is known as meditation. Meditation is both an ancient art and a modern-day skill. There are many meditation techniques and methods from various philosophies and disciplines, but the essence of them all is to quieten and focus the mind. The mind is designed to think and, in fact, the word meditation has the Latin root *meditare* – to think or ponder. Many people say that they cannot meditate because they are unable to 'still' the mind. Instead of trying to stop thinking, we can use meditation to direct our thoughts towards a desired state of feeling, such as being peaceful, calm and content. Even a minute spent in this way takes our minds away from negative thoughts and any physical discomfort, leaving us feeling refreshed and clear-thinking.

On a deeper level, meditation is a journey of rediscovery of our inner selves, in particular our innate goodness. It can help us to surface some inner qualities such as love, courage or patience, which can strengthen and nurture us on every level. As we draw on these inner strengths, we become more self-reliant. We are less likely to be overwhelmed when things get tough, or be unduly influenced by others. This psychological strength becomes the basis for a self-respect that is tangible and enduring, rather than artificial or temporary. It brings about an enhanced sense of well-being and meaning to life.

Finding peace fosters a sense of connection, not only with ourselves but also with other people, communities and the environment. As a spiritual practice, it can connect us with a source of higher energy that some see as a universal guide or as the Divine. The quest to know or connect to the highest spiritual energy comes as a consequence of recognising the depth of our own inner being. The qualities of this energy are often described as 'an ocean of peace', 'unconditional, pure love' and 'light, joy and strength'. Through meditation, and for some through prayer, it is possible to connect to this energy and to experience these qualities within our inner being.

Peace is something we can create in our minds by bringing our thoughts under our conscious control. We know that our thoughts can create feelings in our minds and so we can choose to focus on something positive and uplifting. The most powerful focus is the self and, in particular, the peaceful qualities and goodness at the core of the self. By *thinking* deeply about our original nature as beings of peace, love and wisdom, we can begin to *experience* those qualities that may have been latent or hidden. This moves us towards the calm and silent centre of the inner self. We may experience a powerful sense of stillness and wonder as we discover this peaceful place. With time and practice, this inner peaceful world will become familiar, like a sanctuary, safe home or retreat.

Connecting to our inner peacefulness does not require you to be physically still. In fact, repetitive, everyday activities like walking, washing up and preparing food can form the basis for focusing on peace. Rather than feeling bored and wishing the time away, we can use these kinds of tasks to bring ourselves fully into the present moment, but detached from any noise and bustle around us. As a result, any sense of 'drudgery' disappears and our energy is revitalised.

It is worth pointing out that as you practise bringing peaceful thoughts and images into your mind, it is very common for unwanted thoughts to pop up. Treat your mind as you would a small child who is distracted or misbehaving. Keep guiding it gently back to your desired focus, again and again. In time, you will find that you can experience brief moments of stillness and silence between your thoughts. This is the essence of discovering peace.

Benefits of discovering peace

Physical:

- boosts physical resilience and improves sleep
- reduces experience of pain and discomfort

Emotional:

- reduces anxiety, fear and stress
- induces feelings of calm and coping

Mental:

- improves mental clarity, creativity and focus
- enhances decision-making and problem-solving

Spiritual:

- develops self-knowledge
- promotes feelings of peace, contentment and spiritual connection

Reflections

Recently, after getting up, I have begun to start my day by spending 15 minutes in silence. Because I have been asleep, my mind isn't so busy at this time and I can go deep inside myself. I just watch how I am and accept my thoughts and feelings as they come up. Sometimes, everything becomes balanced and calm and I get a wonderful sensation of connection with myself at a deep level. I feel my inner strength and I seem to go through the day with more ease and confidence, shrugging off things that might otherwise have upset me.

Since I began to recover from depression, I've taken up embroidery. I find I get totally absorbed in the process – the colours of the threads, the shapes and textures which begin to form. I then begin to feel a real sense of quiet and stillness inside, which leaves me feeling I can cope with life. I can also feel this peacefulness when I listen to my favourite music. I imagine peace flowing through my body in gentle waves and it leaves me refreshed and calm.

Before I go to bed I go and sit in a quiet place for a few minutes. I sit in the darkness and focus on my breath going in and out, until my mind begins to calm down. I begin to think of myself as a peaceful and loving being. I then

7

imagine a connection between myself and a greater source of peace which can shower me with a loving light. I picture sending some of this good energy out into the world, to people who may need it.

How to practise discovering peace

 ## CD track

Create a special place to visit and discover peace whenever you want to by listening to the following track:

CD 2 Track 4: A peaceful place (14 mins)

A peaceful day

Start the day by visualising a positive, peaceful day. You can do this before you are even out of bed, or give yourself some quiet time as early as you can.

Begin by relaxing your body using the relaxation practice on page 29, and close your eyes. Begin to imagine a day that begins peacefully, a day that goes so very well. What is it like to start off feeling completely relaxed and enthusiastic about the day ahead?

Whatever you need to do in your day, imagine that any family, friends, colleagues or others around you are calm and peaceful and you feel this way too. How do you see and hear your interactions with others? What words are you using? How does this make you feel? Notice how your day unfolds easily and smoothly as you remain peaceful and at ease.

In such a day, you make time to take a break or to do something for your own well-being. Perhaps you go for a walk, meet a friend or simply enjoy your own company. How does this make you feel? Now see yourself back at home – relaxing and feeling peaceful.

Envisage the end of the day approaching, and see yourself allowing yourself time to reflect on how much you enjoyed the peace of that day. As you go to sleep, what is your last thought?

7

Now bring your attention back to your body and your surroundings, and open your eyes.

A peaceful anchor

Spend a few minutes using the images and sensations you created when you listened to 'A peaceful place' to create a peaceful anchor.

1. When you feel fully relaxed, remember the sights, sounds and sensations this peaceful place evokes. Enjoy the peaceful feelings that arise. As they grow stronger, bring a thumb and forefinger together and squeeze gently for a few seconds. Then let them go and just drift for a minute or two.

2. Next, return to your peaceful scene and re-evoke the images and peaceful feelings. As they grow stronger, again bring that thumb and forefinger together and squeeze gently for a few seconds. Then let them go and just drift again for a minute or two.

3. Repeat the sequence with thumb and forefinger one last time.

You have now 'anchored' your peaceful feelings to a simple physical movement of squeezing thumb and forefinger together. You can use this anchor whenever you feel disturbed or anxious. Just bring your thumb and forefinger together and squeeze gently to rediscover peace.

Moments of well-being

Go into silence

Find a space and time for silence each day, just to stop and rest the body, calm the emotions and quieten the mind. This can foster a sense of peacefulness and inner stability.

Take a break

Take a regular break from whatever you are doing, just for a minute, and focus on peaceful thoughts or images. You will find that when you resume your activity, you will bring to it a clearer mental focus, renewed energy and a more balanced perspective.

Stop for a moment

If you feel that you are too busy or getting 'over-emotional', or that things are getting out of control – stop. Physically stop what you are doing, take a few deep breaths, then breathe slowly. Put a 'full stop' to your thoughts, and a brake on your emotions. Say to yourself, 'I am calm' and then feel the calmness in your body. When you are ready, carry on with your day.

Observe nature

Remember how it feels when you see something that is particularly beautiful in nature, like a special sunset or a vista of bluebells. It brings that feeling of contentment and peace that seems to fill your whole being.

There may be many times each day when we can look at nature's quiet beauty, whether it is a tree, flower or stone, or the way the light comes through a window. Remember to take time when you see such beauty to just appreciate it – be still, look and listen. Hold it in your awareness. You will definitely feel more peaceful for it.

Find unexpected peace

When you find yourself in a traffic jam, your train is late or you are kept waiting for an appointment, instead of getting annoyed use the time to quieten your mind. You can say to yourself, 'this is good, now I can have a bit of peace to myself'. Then allow your body to relax and be comfortable, any upsetting feelings to dissolve, and your thoughts to slow down. Even when you are kept waiting for a short time, you can use those moments to regain your balance and find a sense of inner calm and peace.

Make 'me time'

Finding time for yourself to relax and reflect throughout a day is an important way of sustaining an inner peacefulness. Think about your typical day and plan when such a time could be. It may be going for a walk, having a shower or engaging in an activity that gives you a space to be peaceful.

Plan spaces between activities, time to reflect, daydream, stop and be still – time for doing nothing but enjoying being peaceful.

7

Absorb the mind

Getting absorbed in a quiet activity like sewing, painting or reading can still the thinking mind and bring a deep sense of peace.

Get in the zone

Many people who practise sports report that they find a still zone within themselves when they are in the rhythm of the activity they are doing. This brings them a deep sense of peace and being 'at one' with themselves and everything around them. It does not have to be an extreme sport; any repetitive exercise like cycling, swimming or walking can take you 'into the zone'.

Enjoy music

Some music is able to transport us to a space that is deeply calm and can fill us with a sense of peace. Listening to music, singing or playing an instrument are all ways of nurturing inner peace and a sense of spiritual connection.

Personal plan for well-being

Once you have tried some of the tools in this guide, you might want to return to the well-being audit you completed at the beginning, where you shaded in the wheel of well-being (see page 18). To help you to develop a plan for enhancing your well-being, reflect on the following questions:

⊛ Has my overall rating of my sense of well-being improved?

⊛ Are there any particular positive changes in my well-being (physical, emotional, mental, spiritual) that I have noticed already? How have these happened (eg. from using a particular tool or activity)?

⊛ Which of the tools would I like to bring into my life or practise some more?

⊛ What benefits do I hope to gain?

Now use any ideas you have developed while working through the tools in this guide, together with your reflections on the above questions, to make a well-being plan. Begin by 'signing up' to three changes you are going to make. Anything you put into the plan should be realistic, achievable and 'measurable', that is, you need to know when and whether you have achieved it. Be as specific about the detail as you can. By avoiding biting off more than you can chew and focusing on something you can change in a small space of time, you will experience success quickly. Each small step you achieve will give you the positive feelings and self-confidence to take another step. Before long, you will be climbing energetically up the ladder of well-being and gaining a wonderful view from the top!

From time to time, return to the well-being wheel and rate your overall well-being levels again, noticing any progress you have made. If you have slipped down a level on any dimension, be sure to take note of this and ask yourself why. Use the tools in this guide that seem most useful to redress the balance.

My well-being plan

The change I wish to make	How will it look/feel and what difference will it make?	How will I do it?	When will I do it?	What support will I need to do it (and to get over any obstacles in the way)?
1.				
2.				
3.				

Going forwards

We hope you have enjoyed this book and the CDs. Even if you have tried just one or two tools or listened to some of the CD tracks, the positive energy they create will go with you into all areas of your life. You may find yourself being able to stand back and notice what is happening around you from a more detached perspective. You will then find it easier to respond in a positive and resourceful way.

As challenging situations come up, you may wish to go back to some of the tools that can help you to prepare for these, such as *Use your imagination* (Tool 2) or *Think positively* (Tool 3).

If you have time on your hands, give yourself permission to do something creative (Tool 4), treat yourself to some self-nurturing (Tool 6) or relax (Tool 1), just for the sake of it. If you only have a minute, use it to go into silence and peace (Tool 7). If you only have a few seconds, a smile or laugh will give you and others a helpful boost (Tool 5). Before you realise it, you will have put all seven tools into practice!

Above all, keep visualising yourself in a state of optimum well-being and you will find yourself moving towards that goal.

We wish you well on your journey.

About the The Janki Foundation

The Janki Foundation for Global Health Care is a UK-based healthcare charity dedicated to positive human development. Drawing on research demonstrating that positive states of mind promote health and healing, it has developed a unique personal and team development programme in support of healthcare professionals, called *Values in Healthcare: a spiritual approach.*

Lifting Your Spirits is a self-help companion guide that has been developed specifically for patients and those coping with illness, including carers.

The Heart of Well-being is a further companion guide that has been developed for anyone who is concerned to support and improve their own well-being.

Together, these materials support a whole-person approach to healthcare, an approach that considers the needs of patients, carers, healthcare practitioners and others at all levels of body, mind and spirit.

For further information about these Janki Foundation initiatives and the training opportunities available, please contact:

The Janki Foundation for Global Health Care
449-451 High Road, London NW10 2JJ
United Kingdom
T +44 (0)20 8459 1400/9090
F +44 (0)20 8459 9091
E info@jankifoundation.org
W www.jankifoundation.org

About the British Holistic Medical Association

Formed in 1983 by a group of medical doctors and students, the BHMA is a public-professional network of like-minded people – mainstream healthcare professionals, CAM practitioners, and members of the public – committed to promoting holistic practice in healthcare, and holistic well-being in individuals and communities.

BHMA
PO Box 371
Bridgwater
Somerset TA6 9BG
United Kingdom
T +44 (0)1278 722 000
E admin@bhma.org
W www.bhma.org

Personal well-being notes

Personal well-being notes

Personal well-being notes

Personal well-being notes